COALS
FROM
the Altar

LONNETTA RAGLAND

COALS FROM THE ALTAR: A POETIC JOURNEY OF FAITH AND REVELATION by Lonnetta R. Ragland
Published by Lonnetta R. Ragland
thecoals7@gmail.com

This book or parts thereof may not be reproduced in any form, stored in a retrieval system, or transmitted in any form by any means—electronic, mechanical, photocopy, recording, or otherwise—without prior written permission of the publisher, except as provided by United States of America copyright law.

Unless otherwise noted, all Scripture quotations are taken from are from the King James Version of the Bible.

Scripture quotations marked NKJV are taken from the New King James Version®. Copyright © 1982 by Thomas Nelson. Used by permission. All rights reserved.

Scripture quotations marked NLT are from the Holy Bible, New Living Translation, copyright © 1996,

Copyright © 2021 by Lonnetta R. Ragland
All rights reserved

International Standard Book Number: 978-1-7338730-7-9
E-book ISBN: 978-1-7338730-8-6

While the author has made every effort to provide accurate internet addresses at the time of publication, neither the publisher nor the author assumes any responsibility for errors or for changes that occur after publication. Further, the publisher does not have any control over and does not assume any responsibility for author or third-party websites or their content.

21 22 23 24 25 — 9 8 7 6 5 4 3 2 1
Printed in the United States of America

CONTENTS

ACKNOWLEDGMENTS *ix*

PREFACE: Go *xi*

I: CONFRONTATION

4 a.m. *1*

Silk *2*

Face to Face *3*

Audacity *4*

The Question That Remains *5*

Good Night *6*

Dear Love *7*

Annual Review *8*

Deadly Comfort *9*

COALS FROM THE *Altar*

Cabin Pressure *10*

Penned Consolidation *11*

Indigestion *13*

Sleepwalking *14*

The Response *16*

Like a Glove *17*

Reflection *18*

Walking Out *19*

The War Within *20*

Unmoved *22*

The Shift *23*

Poetic Deliverance—Looking Back to Move Forward *24*

Finish Strong *27*

New Season *28*

II: TRANSFORMATION

Point of the Prompt *31*

Moiety *32*

Waiting for the Call *33*

Faith *34*

Eternal Pursuit *35*

NOW *37*

Sunday's Best *38*

On the Table *39*

Self-Discovery *41*

Inspired *42*

Thirty Thousand Feet *43*

Champion *44*

Heart Transfer *45*

Yes, You *46*

Ears to Hear *48*

Her Legacy *49*

Irreplaceable *50*

Resting in His Arms *52*

III: REVELATION

The Children with Burning Hearts *55*

YHWH *56*

Partout *57*

Horizon *58*

Relentless *59*

Harmony in a Dry Place *60*

At Dawn *61*

Garden Regeneration *62*

Abba *63*

Extol *64*

Exclusive *65*

Indigo Bridges *66*

Love's Stage *68*

No Comparison *69*

Sup with Me *70*

A Psalm for the One *71*

In the Event Of... *73*

EPILOGUE *75*

ABOUT THE AUTHOR *77*

ACKNOWLEDGMENTS

Thank You to the Father, Son, and Holy Spirit for being my coauthor and inspiration! I could not and would not have been able to do this without You. You are the God who speaks and desires to be known by Your people. On this journey in faith thus far, You've not only revealed more of Yourself to me, but also challenged me to see myself the way You see me.

You've given me courage, creativity, and so much more to bring *Coals from the Altar* to life. And now I dedicate it right back to You. Though words cannot express what You mean to me, *Coals from the Altar* is my humble attempt.

Signed,
Your daughter, and nothing less

PREFACE

This is a book about the significance of introspection and expression.

It's about being honest with yourself—about your past, what you've done, and what has been done to you.

It's not about playing the blame game but rather taking responsibility and learning how to forgive out of the forgiveness Christ makes available to us.

It's about healing and cleaning out the house of your life in preparation for the future.

It's about discovering who you really are and the various parts of the journey it takes us to get there.

It's about finding your voice and breaking free from cycles of sin's bondage to walking in freedom.

It's about receiving the abundant love of our incomparable heavenly Father.

It's about you and me and the collective lessons we learn along the way.

It's about Him and us and the path to His embrace.

GO

But I am too young,
    and possess nothing to teach the wise.
Their silver streaks eclipse my potential;
    they traversed earth's terrain long before my lungs
    learned to respire.

My words lack eloquence
    and stutter like Morse code.
Conveying thoughts and feelings
    is like running backwards submerged in the aquatic.
How will I speak for You
    when I can barely speak for myself?
My lips unclean,
    and surrounded by the same.
Who will listen to anything that comes from this flawed
    vessel?
    Unworthy to speak Your name.

Realizations of inadequacy are flooding
    and all that's left is to plunge prostrate.
Disposition interrupted;
    and I am overcome.
Here am I
    speechless and unqualified.

Yet the King of Kings who sits high,
    looked low to touch my lips.
Opened my mouth
    and promised to fill it.
Warned against fear of their eyes
    and vowed to be with me.
Commanded me to speak
    whether they listen or not.

I.

Confrontation

I sought the LORD, and He heard me, and delivered me from all my fears.

—Psalm 34:4, NKJV

4 A.M.

Slumbering eyes burst open and
    lips slowly part outside of my control.
A whisper escapes,
    "Why did you stop?"
Percolating thoughts travel back in time
    and vacation there.
They finally return,
    but not empty handed.
Packed inside the visiting memory
    was an opposing question.
Another whisper escapes,
    "Why did I begin?"

Born with an attraction to linguistic gymnastics and
    a lexicon that locked me into quiet captivity.
Silence plagued my orifice,
    while each word I wrote illustrated a progressing life
    portrait.
Writing gave voice to voicelessness and
    captured growing pains and frailty.
It caught me,
    when I fell.
It accepted me
    when I couldn't.
It refused to let me walk through life numb,
    and still, I abandoned it.

Distracted by grown-up time snatchers,
    careers, bills and chronic writer's block.

Yet today, here I stand,
    extending an olive branch.
Hoping to reunite with my pen and prose
    between these lines.

SILK

These arms hold tunnels,
    linking your story to mine.
Crimson cells flowing through veins with vitality,
    overcoming billy-club laws beating tirelessly for end of day.

Seas of onyx wave to the heavens
    with burning bellows for deliverance.
Scowling hands race to silence,
    but devilish fools can't hear emerald refrains.
Brilliance shines in these resilient eyes,
    and mystery is embedded in cheekbones of smiles.
Joy and pain embrace,
    giving birth to tears of diamond determination.

The land of our mother
    adorns us like the finest silk.
So straighten that neck upright, chile;
    activate that royal mind.
Breathe a life of inimitable melodies,
    and never lose sight of your jewels.

LONNETTA RAGLAND

FACE TO FACE

Come a little closer.
    Yes, that's it.
Feel free...
    just feel free.
Leave the pressure in the cabin,
    delegate the rush to the waves.

Come a little closer,
    closer still.
Dance your eyes in syncopated rhythm,
    atop redwood canopies.
Envision with your lips ruby strawberries and electric
    rainbows,
    and plant your feet for an interlude.

Closer,
    a little more.
Hearken
    like stargazers at full bloom.
Surrender
    each breath drawing you into dimensions filled with
    velvet clouds.

Come a little closer,
    and tell me your name.
The heavens know who you are,
    but do you?

Coals from the Altar

AUDACITY

Searching for acceptance
   like a foxhound in hot pursuit,
Laying down hopes and dreams
   to keep pace with this marathon,
Beautifying faces
   with rotating camouflage,
Judging above rank
   deciding guilt and innocence,
Stepping on heads
   to get ahead,
Disillusioned
   by me-centric mentalities,
Energetically shuffling
   productive as a train stuck in reverse,
Blinded
   by scales that taint line of sight,
Suffocating
   from darkness convinced it's light,
Cherishing comfort
   in comfort zone,
Tossing bodies
   as if for sport,
Striving for truth
   outside of Truth Himself,
Spinning impulsively
   in stagnation,
Crying out to hollow statues,
   desperate for answers they can't give,

Consequently deafened
   to the knock at heart's door
And when crisis shakes the ground on which we stand,
   we audaciously petition God to fix it on demand.

LONNETTA RAGLAND

THE QUESTION THAT REMAINS

Speaking never ceases,
    but diverting attentions clog their ears.

Bellowing tones as if they would move mountains,
    they miss the call for communion.

Universally centered in omnipresence,
    while their zooming feet miss the point.

Patiently waiting with mercy on the right
    yet they rotate wheels around righteous judgement at the left.

Being the all and all that is ever needed,
    they test instead of tasting and seeing.

Sitting upon a throne of certified faithfulness,
    they pulsate for the lesser, propelling offensive aromas on high.

Commanding time written on the clock's weary hands,
    they face the two divergent paths of this age.

Extended arms of unfailing love makes their acquaintance,
    holding invitation to choose this day whom they will serve.

COALS FROM THE *Altar*

GOOD NIGHT

subtle winds vacillate
   while leaves rustle.
light rays dance
   and the earth's floor is an astute mate.

the warmth of the day
   caresses my countenance
yet on this journey,
   there are multiple options at stake.

nature's characters banter endlessly;
   each clamoring for the main stage.
they are too occupied for my plight,
   so I cower from asking for their opinion.

all the while, the sun is being rocked to sleep by the
   towering sapphire,
   and the moon will soon come to tuck him in.
clock hands revolving,
   but still, am I.

LONNETTA RAGLAND

DEAR LOVE...

It's
   official.
It's
   been inscribed on the onyx amidst infinite stars.
With just a glimpse of you,
   I feel the weight of what's at stake.
The cost is high,
   but belief holds that the reward will surpass.
I've
   heard about you.
I've
   sung about you.
I've
   tried to hide my feelings about you.
Thought I saw you around the way,
   once or twice.
Tried to envision life through your eyes,
   and where I thought you might be, I decided to reside.
I dreamed of what you would look like when we finally met—
   warm hues of kaleidoscope sunsets.
I imagined us above uplifting waves of hope,
   sailing on a catamaran built with enough faith to
   withstand the rain.
I vowed to learn from past lessons
   and persevere forward with a renewed heart.

Finally, you respond in a cashmere utterance,
   summoning me to look up.
For who love is and will always be
   lies in the heavenly Father above.
I did what you said,
   I implored to encounter all of you.
Yet between you and I
   still exists infinite epochs and galaxies.

Coals from the Altar

ANNUAL REVIEW

Yes to Him,
    meant no to him.
It was an aggressive transaction
    that shattered cycle of indecision.
The more tears and prayers invested,
    the greater the profit yielded.
I put it all on the line
    and gained a new level of currency.
I sought the heavenly system of checks and balances
    and accounts are overflowing.
I can now give
    and not just borrow.

Heaven's securities and exchange commission negotiated
    the whole deal—
        trading my bonds for a free market economy.

LONNETTA RAGLAND

DEADLY COMFORT

Your neck snaps back
    and eyes flame with offense.
Your chest balloons
    and sigh rattles the curtains.

Would you rather
    I watch you walk toward the cliff
    in silence?

Would you prefer
    I standby in glee as you cross the intersection
    and not warn of the danger speeding your way?

Would you be more comfortable
    if I nodded in agreement to your plans
    of socialized irreverence?

In a time when kingdom will come,
    why do you mislabel love as judgment?
In a day when one choice impacts eternity,
    will you remember your squandered inheritance?
In a place where the veil split,
    can you perceive what was given to you?

Would you rather I cheer from the sidelines
    as you play a game where death is the immortal prize?

COALS FROM THE *Altar*

CABIN PRESSURE

Heart races
  in competition with thoroughbreds.
Hands shut
  like a bear trap that achieved the day's quota.
Silence permeates.

Desperation cries
  prayers for redemption only God can hear.
Collective swims
  anxious, while sweat beads on brows of all shades.
Demand percolates.

Mind melts
  smart, like hot wax.
Neurotransmitters chase
  fleeting scenarios in overdrive.
Peace resonates.

LONNETTA RAGLAND

PENNED CONSOLIDATION

Surrounded by their good intentions,
    famished hearts
    and faultless restrictions.

Their green eyes watched me shrink;
    saturating my view with disillusionment
    while their expectations pushed me to the cliff's brink.

Their therapist, I never failed to empathize,
    relentlessly fed obese egos
    as they ignored my encouragement to exercise.

Transformed myself into their safe place to hide,
    a jovial shelter
    or transport when they needed a ride.

This became my unofficial obligation —
    worn like a badge
    until I suffered heart breaking penetration.

Overnight I underwent a surgical divide,
    suffered metamorphosis during operation,
    from one to two lives destined to collide.

So we played our fractions
    and danced in exoteric accolades,
    foxtrotting vessels moving fast but making no traction.

Their eyes and ears still marveled at the sounds I spoke,
    ignorant of my authentic voice—
    never brave enough to evoke.

Lies became staunch reality,
    and reality became devoted lies.
The seesaw depleted every part of me.

And through the fire has been my pen,
honorable, even when others conspire;
   a nonjudgmental listener and friend.

We meet here at a point of expressive consolidation,
   as we transform from a separate two
   and I become a single articulation.

LONNETTA RAGLAND

INDIGESTION

Failed by the one
    whose sole responsibility was not to.
He is half of the reason I am here,
    yet downplayed position on the sidelines.
In the absence of action,
    verbalized silence.
Delegated responsibility
    to them.
Set no credo,
    and provided no parameters.
Illustrated aim's opposite
    and backed down in the face of the smallest extension
    of him.
He saw Goliath
    and didn't fight for me.
Dropped me,
    yet carried on.
His mouth uttering restrained words
    in delinquent sprinkles of appeasement.
Retroactive payment for shouldas, wouldas, couldas
    in place of acknowledging this reality.
Meanwhile, he's blessed each day
    with another chance to make things right.
Instead his eyes plead the 5th
    while his belly bloats with four hundred and forty-four
    months of muted regret.

And I accept the apology that I may never receive
    and I choose to forgive.

COALS FROM THE *Altar*

SLEEPWALKING

Glazed eyes
    staggered to the left and to the right.
I investigated my soul
    like a detective for clues.
Cried out for assistance
    but no one comprehended.
It was time to leave this place
    but only found maps with dubious directions.

As my feet pounded the icy pavement,
    my soles were shocked with alarming sensation.
Halted in bewilderment
    and now facing a fork in the road with signs I could not see.
Under poised surface,
    an earthquake shook every perception.
Sensed volumes of ancient prayers prayed
    and answered in a millisecond.

Like a bolt of lightning
    I was struck by a voice.
The words shot arrows at the one I loved most
    and called for a sacrificial choice:

"This may be what you think you want,
    but My dear child,
    it is not what you need.
It's killing you softly
    in your sleep.
While you saunter in darkness,
    you're drowning in idolatry."

Like a ship being anchored,
    so was my heart's center,

LONNETTA RAGLAND

Newfound consciousness steadied me;
    to accept this confrontation was not my fight.
My fists dropped in surrendered humility
    and indomitable trust.
I laid down the sacrifice.
    Awakened.

Coals from the Attar

THE RESPONSE

When your feet pivot left and
    He wants them to amble right

When you want to remain here and
    He says the hour has come to go there

When your hands hoard and
    He wants you to give

When you are flooded with certainty and
    He constructs an enflamed stop sign

When your norm is to speak your mind and
    He calls you to still your lips

When you want to casually sleep in and
    He wants you to rise early to converse with Him

When you have plans and
    He asks you to make Him your priority

When you are around your friends and
    He wants to join

When you want to control every room in the house of your life and
    He waits for you to make Him Lord of each one...

How will you answer?

LONNETTA RAGLAND

LIKE A GLOVE

Fit like a glove
  yesterday.
Embraced me hospitably
  with fabrics made to protect from harm.
Warmed me temperately
  during frigid conditions.
Cradled me gently
  with time-bound perfection.
A closer read of the manufacture's label revealed
  a hidden feature to separate hands from joining in
  reverent communion.
Fit like a glove yesterday;
  today it didn't.

COALS FROM THE *Altar*

REFLECTION

If you told me sunflowers could grow in a dark room,
    I'd plant them with anticipation.

If your compass directed me in circles,
    I'd follow until we reached our destination.

If you questioned my loyalty,
    I'd answer with more attention.

If you showed me your true colors,
    I'd focus on my favorite ones.

If I would get alone for at least one hour and 26 minutes at the Genesis of my day,
    I'd be able to perceive my true reflection.

LONNETTA RAGLAND

WALKING OUT

Fashioned protective walls
  out of metal bars.
The unpadded box spring mattress,
  a cradle of iniquity.
Had a little desk,
  on which I placed pictures of me smiling.
I didn't want to forget
  what I used to look like.
The guards of temptation
  became my confidants.
Meaningless chatter from neighbors
  distracted my thoughts.
Solo
  in here.
Decorated
  it the best I could.
Made
  it feel like home.
Anticipated
  scheduled meals and grey yard time.
Ran
  free within limits of fenced in detention.
Confinement
  became my comfort zone.
Caught in a numbed gaze
  until interrupted by an illuminated figure in white.
Too far to see lucidly,
  but I was drawn to the glorious light.
My feet began to march in that direction,
  while swaddled in a protective permission to let it all go.
He spoke a word of redemption to me
  and I surrendered.
He embraced my brokenness
  and called me daughter.

COALS FROM THE *Altar*

THE WAR WITHIN

She
  is my only competition.

I
  see her back there.
Smiling superficially,
  misguided.
Prancing on roadside
  with idol feet.
Different faces for different situations,
  with dormant dread of being known.
Screaming with a muted cry,
  searching with no aim.
Members disassociated while unified,
  passively inviting heartbreaking isolation.
Faculties suffocating in an enclosed chamber,
  lodged with devil's pie.

Parentage in adolescence,
  responsibilities bestowed before her time.
Heir of pedigree
  of motley falsehoods disguised as wisdom.
Mastered camouflage,
  mirror marred by beautiful deception.
Independent of wholeness,
  void and unaware.

Exposed,
  but hidden.
Started,
  but unfinished.
Ignorant of the Refiner's fire,
  thus, a non-existent seek.

LONNETTA RAGLAND

Warmed by the knock at her heart's entrance,
    she hears her name pronounced like never before.
This voice,
    This presence shattered her consciousness in an instant.

Once lost,
    now found.
Once captive,
    now released.
You see that girl over there?
    She used to be me.

COALS FROM THE *Altar*

UNMOVED

Sun rays
   drip on left cheek.
Familiar conjecture
   traces circles around the right.

Here
   I am.

Glistening curtains
   cover the day's doors.
Knobs escaped undetected
   in the shadows.
Before chosen,
   bamboozled blue.
Moans fall
   from reticent skies.
Rough air scrapes
   these weary windows.
Condensation forms,
   and whimpers at my feet.
Vast terrain
   limited by partner gatekeepers.
Yet able to behold
   I am still here.

LONNETTA RAGLAND

THE SHIFT

Descaled vision
    discover delinquent goodbyes.
Hamster wheel cycles
    of normalized insanity.
Stagnated dedication
    to diminished sobriety.

Gazing up to theatrical contradictions,
    stuck in child's pose.
Crystalized mental snapshots of rage,
    models of divergent roles.

Combatting love,
    left paths to be discerned in clarified ambiguity.
Love,
    a misinterpreted phenom.
Camouflaged,
    until You.

COALS FROM THE *Altar*

POETIC DELIVERANCE: LOOKING BACK TO MOVE FORWARD

Been reading my old contemplations
    from juvenile yester-years.
Eight frayed notebooks brimming with daily chronicles
    from playground to campus.
Digesting them all took some time
    and also pick-pocketed my breath.
Captivated
    as if reading jaw dropping fiction.
There was newness present with each chapter,
    as if this was not my own life's rendition.

The present rapidly became the past
    and their memories subconsciously suppressed.
Privately transcribed so long ago,
    within once comforting lines.

Just a little girl
    who studied how to cut with lyrics from the kindred classroom.
Learned how to resolve conflict
    modeled by detachment.
Learned what the grown folk do at night
    from squeaky professors.
Learned the whole and naught
    about how I should expect to be loved and give it in return.

Role models filled my senses
    with rhythms that gave my hips power.
And took care of myself and the little one who followed
    during momma's night shift.

LONNETTA RAGLAND

Learned early on to depend on a device for protection
    from robbers that might lurk.

Scanning the land for adoration
    and heading in the wrong direction to find it.
Smiling on the outside,
    and fragmenting internally.
Gamboling blindly,
    sinking deeper in transgressions,
It was dark and messy;
    in no one could I confide.
Self-reliantly taught myself how to cope,
    to journal and poeticize.

These pages drip with torment,
    seeking attention to define a lacking identity.
In search thereof,
    I played the game before it played me.
Accepted spirit of independence
    and the world's definition of who it said I should be.
I laid it all on the line
    for love's possibility.
Award-worthy performance enacted
    theatrical production adorned with silver lined simplicity.
Behind the scenes immorality invited shame,
    and shame led to hiding.
Hiding birthed lies
    and the lies paved way for me to lose myself in myself.

These pages exposed veiled bondage
    and necessity for repentance.
Now
    the healing journey can begin.
No longer dripping with pain,
    these pages are covered in redemption.
Grace kept my past from
    resulting in death's sentence.

Coals from the Altar

Refused to let me suffer
    sins' full consequence.
Elated He heard my screams for help
    even when I didn't have a voice.

LONNETTA RAGLAND

FINISH STRONG

Breast-stroking against the currant,
    each one like eleven.
Time passes with inexorable expanse,
    becoming an abhorred pastime.
While motion endures,
    these weary eyes strain ahead.
Privilege of querying amputated;
    replaced by one possibility.
Obligated to keep my head in the game,
    and above the waves.
Revelation strikes like lightening,
    and effaces distraction of the passersby.
In the rear,
    defeat extends salutation.
That imp transforms into an anchor,
    and beckons me to sink.
An intensified refusal to give up
    surged my reservoir.
No time for sinking legs,
    the future is awaiting my arrival.

Coals from the *Altar*

NEW SEASON

Foliage negotiate fluttering hues
   and summersault to the terra firma.
Fahrenheit indicators follow suit
   as the days race to the finish line.
Clouds bully the skyscraping blue
   and kidnap summer's shadows.
Classic order of events
   on a rhythmic timetable.

Immaculate thrusts imperceptible
   unlock ogles stare.
Sharp edges in power
   and pigments like auburn, apricots and cinnamon
   illuminated.
Brisk sounds in tune
   reveal silenced may-day sirens.
Time elapses
   and the dam erodes.
Gushing fire hydrant waterworks
   pound bruises through the atmospheric chest.
Regret flashes between the tree pyramids
   attempting to plug root systems.
Clarity anew imparts revelation
   and election to surrender.

Nature witnesses this cycle
   become an untouched season.

II.

Transformation

Therefore, if anyone is in Christ, he is a new creature; the old things passed away; behold, new things have come.

—2 Corinthians 5:17

POINT OF THE PROMPT

About face,
    there is no turning back.
Like the unstoppable hands of grandfather's chronometer
    tick-tocking forward in wisdom is the only option.
Like the chime that strikes our ears at mid-day and
    midnight,
    so our Savior appeals to our hearts for an invitation.
Our response determines what happens
    or doesn't.
Will we let Him take us to higher heights
    and beyond the extraordinary?
Or keep ticking along
    like we never heard a sound?

MOIETY

In search of me,
    I traveled unpaved roads.
Beckoned by a part of me
    foreign to me.
I followed obscure trails illuminated
    through towering branches.
Their leaves sheltered
    during raging storms in the blackest of nights.
Lightning tethered,
    severing attachment to everything once known.
Thunder pounded
    my desire to go where I wanted.
Rain washed
    away pride.

In search of my voice,
    alone.
I braced for impact in the wilderness of change
    and bereaved the order of yesterday.
Gales blew to the west,
    and disrobed everything I owned.
Nothing held value any longer
    outside the purpose of this quest.
Vantage point reconfigured
    and I couldn't unsee what I'd seen.

Found what I didn't know I was searching for,
    a love that declared I'd arrived.
And a still, quiet part of me
    released the sweetest song with lyrics I could never have composed on my own.

LONNETTA RAGLAND

WAITING FOR THE CALL

Journeying on the unbounded
    to an undiscovered destination.
Down this road I travel,
    without proper navigation.
Possible routes
    outnumber April showers.
Paused at the fork
    to avoid taking a wrong turn.
If God wants me to follow,
    He'll make sure I understand His direction, right?
As time passes,
    nothing is more important than this wait.

COALS FROM THE *Altar*

FAITH

My soul strains for a glimpse
   on a chockablock avenue.

Curiosity intensifies
   and incites receptivity for a momentous pursuit.

Suddenly, You reveal Yourself
   before I could find You.

Motionless in awe-induced reticence,
   I plummet at Your hallowed feet

In the presence of the Author and Finisher of my faith,
   I couldn't find suitable words to speak.

The ability to communicate is misplaced,
   and vanished are the phrases used previously to impress.

I sensed He only desired one,
   and my fidelity-filled will shouted yes!

LONNETTA RAGLAND

ETERNAL PURSUIT

One encounter
   has left me struggling to lyrically express.
How can I justly describe
   the consuming fire of Your presence?

An eternal decision is made
   and peace subdues.
Now Lord over every area of my life;
   with exceeding joy, I begin this journey with You.

Who I am
   no longer exists outside of who You are.
Your glory draws me in,
   leading me like the north star.

My core constricts
   in humble adoration.
Heart beats accelerate
   while knees bow in liberating submission.

Orifice loads up the ammo
   and spews out aggressive rounds of repentance.
Empty chambers lay motionless,
   in desperate need of Your forgiveness.

It is, You are,
   this is all too much for me to ascertain.
Principal paradigm wrecked
   and stirred so far outside of its native lane.
Straightaway I see...
   to see You requires a different set of eyes.
Doubt abruptly efforts to cloud my vision
   so I dump it roadside.

COALS FROM THE Altar

You, O God, are so God;
    more existent than the letters on this page.
Spirit yearns to capture the meet that now marks me;
    together we'll play out the rest on life's theatrical stage.

Yet at this moment,
    this poet is left speechless.
Determined to find the attributes
    to describe that which is indescribable by any earthly genius.

The credence of Your truth
    has awakened a treasure trove of energy.
Hence, I will spend the rest of my days searching for ways
    to translate what You mean to me.
Because I realize You want to do even more
    for the one reading this elegy.

LONNETTA RAGLAND

NOW

Twelve thousand seven hundred seventy-five days
   of life.
And today
   I experienced breath for the first time.
There's the past and there's the future.
   but what about now?

Time to advance from then and
   retract premature steps into the eventual.
Dare I sway with the rhythm
   of this moment.
The slow rise
   and the gradual fall.
In the beat in my chest,
   discovered the Light in the Darkness.
The source of my respiration,
   the orchestrator of cardiac pulse.

In this present moment,
   I am here with the Waymaker.
Not behind,
   and not in front.
Revelation surfs this rhythm
   like a tidal wave.
How He has sustained me,
   and continues to love me.
Through each breath,
   and each heartbeat.
Each unsupervised by my attention;
   it was the Miracle Worker all along.
And that same Promise Keeper is still watching over me
   in this present moment.
The only difference is
   now I know.

COALS FROM THE *Altar*

SUNDAY'S BEST

Adorned neck of timidity
    with a scarf made of the most confident moxie.

Wrapped the shrug of her shoulders
    with a shawl embossed with pure emphaticalness.

Poured herself into a mosaic gown,
    perfectly designed to distract from imperfections.

Rocked fire pumps with five-inch heels
    to elevate above history's secrets.

Glossed anti-social lips
    a crimson shade of extroversion.

Exhausted by this masquerade,
    sat on the fence like a bird passing time.

But today her manicured hands took off magenta sunglasses
    to liberate the story in her hazed eyes.

LONNETTA RAGLAND

ON THE TABLE

"God, please heal me."

Deafening silence filled my mind's waiting room,
    until a long-awaited retort whispered,
"Do you want to be made whole?"

A resounding "yes" leaped from my chest,
    before the question could fully register.
His inquiry injected me with rapid willingness,
    thrusting me to pre-op.
Alone...
    with the Creator of all!
Pressured by dubious expectations,
    yet sedated by a peace.
A knowing that I was on the right operating table,
    with the only surgeon who could fix me.
Fearful of the initial incision,
    but willing to endure.

Like a scalpel,
    His parables pruned diseased regions of my anatomy.
Jesus was the Light
    Who pointed to countless areas that needed surgical attention.
And the Holy Spirit was my comforter through it all.

Under His anesthesia,
    I underwent a series of immaculately precise procedures.
Debridement of traumas' scar tissue
    hidden in the deep.
Excision of iniquitous tumors
    compromising vital organs.
Drainage of idol philosophies
    carried through trillions of synapses.

COALS FROM THE *Altar*

Deflated polluted laden lungs,
    and filled them with His will.

I arise with my true ipseity
    absolutely rooted in this Healer.
The face I shall forever seek
    and what He's done for me, I will forever speak.

"Not so fast...
    it is not time to emerge.
This is just the beginning of your transformation."

Thus...
    I laid back down.

LONNETTA RAGLAND

SELF-DISCOVERY

She has a way with words,
    or is it that they have a way with her?
An unlikely kinship
    with no blood bond.
Ever since she could write,
    she wrote.
She found meaning in words
    as she constructed.
Together they created and articulated,
    while filling space between the lines.

Fondness grew
    and they journeyed around the world.

They were stopped in their tracks
    when they encountered one Word that broke down barriers.
They were speechless in awe of this Word
    Who surfaced buried afflictions and then healed them.

This Word
    was like a hammer that broke rocks into pieces.
This Word
    exposed a predestined bond.
Created to tell the story of the One who
    spoke the first.

COALS FROM THE *Altar*

INSPIRED

Spoken.
Inspired.
Written.

To be spoken again
    without end.
Words that hold more power
    than the sun over the deepest night.
Sharper than a sword
    slicing through the finest silk.
The lighthouse
    that warns us of treacherous waters.
The compass
    that points us in the right direction.

Collectively,
    these living words reveal and empower.

Just
    as the One who inspired.
Words
    that are more than words.
Pertinent
    eternally and infinitely essential.

Read
    and meditate.
Ask
    and understand.

Seek
    and find.
Get still,
    and know.

LONNETTA RAGLAND

THIRTY THOUSAND FEET

Tremendous rotations accelerate beneath,
    afore the placid elevation.
Ascending,
    leaving the world behind.
Mesmerized,
    by Your ineffable firmament.

Attention overwhelmed
    by the infinitude of rolling blankets of pallid.
And a canvas of sapphire
    that commands my gaze.
The gift of finding You here
    as I pass through Your celestial grace.

COALS FROM THE *Altar*

CHAMPION

The hour came to speak,
   and a force invisible
     fired countless blows to thwart release.

Rounds of self-condemning expression,
   sparring in the ring of life,
     busted lip knocked out by suppression.

Canary stars dance circles around my crown,
   the will to fight this thief -
     impelled only by the grace that still abounds.

Proliferating muscle fatigue attracts body depletion,
   and discombobulates opponent's appearance –
     he who has already been defeated.

Deemed punch-drunk and powerless,
   now everything stolen illegally,
     he must dispossess.

His lies renounced
   and the glorious might of the Champion,
     will I forever pronounce.

LONNETTA RAGLAND

HEART TRANSFER

Mouths profess,
   yet hearts are so far.
Time diminishes widening distance,
   and births false sense of security.

So close to transformation
   though amuck is a tainted love filter.
Stuck at the dividing wall of submission,
   complacency fills the veiled void.
Feet swift in sightless deception,
   purposed to remain in obscurity.

Souls and mouths yearn for alignment,
   the courage to trust and believe completely.
Scream for course correction,
   cry out for peace.
Choosing to follow Him,
   is refusing to stay the same.
He gives you a clean heart
   as you embrace your new name.

COALS FROM THE *Altar*

YES, YOU

You
   are one of a kind.
Distinctive
   like a snowflake.
Dynamic
   like each sunset.
Yes,
   you.

You,
   who God loves with an unconditional affection.
Overflowing
   reminiscent of the Niagara.
Incomprehensible
   like the primordial pyramids of Egypt.
You,
   whom God knows.
And still,
   loves.

Earth lacks the ink essential
   to express His attributes.
He is not a figment of imagination
   or a hollow statue.
He is more real
   than the ground you are standing on.
He transcends
   your ability to define.
He looks past your faults and wants
   and sees your need.

If only your mirror reflected
   the way God sees you.

LONNETTA RAGLAND

If only your intellect sought
    what He purposed you to do.
He bestows upon you
    the gift of choice.
To make Him Lord over every area of your life
    or worship your own desires in absence of The Light.

EARS TO HEAR

Standing firm in the heavens
    and fastened to eternity.
You sustain my life in the words You impart,
    and I yearn to live.
Bless me again,
    like You did when fresh dew slumbered on the green.

I incline my spirit in anticipation of Your guidance;
    my steps unrealized without it.
Withhold anything
    but never exile me from Your tone.
Hearing what the Captain of my soul has decided about me
    builds my vision for what I cannot perceive.
And despite the temperature of my emotions,
    I choose to believe.

LONNETTA RAGLAND

HER LEGACY

Her life was given new meaning
    the day you entered this world.
The sparkle in her eyes
    and the purpose in her steps.
The delight in her heart
    and the love in her laugh.
She kept you close
    and stretched herself to be everything you needed.
Seems like yesterday,
    she gave your cheek her last kiss.
Too young to stand on your own;
    nothing could have prepared you for this.
As the sun graces the skies with each day anew,
    Her legacy shines brightly through you.

Coals from the Altar

IRREPLACEABLE

(Dedicated to C.L.)

Just because a woman births a child,
    doesn't make her a mother.
It takes an incomprehensible level of love, sacrifice and humility
    and so much more.
It takes the learning of skills often not taught
    instead harvested along the way.
It takes public tests
    and endless choices.
It takes desperate prayers and astounding resilience,
    all while little eyes look up to you in dependency.

Many hats and names,
    though only one captures your true essence.
Thick skin,
    and a fragile heart.
Ready fists
    and a willingness to forgive.
Façades abundant,
    and determined survival.

Hungry,
    but keen to bestow your portion.
Imperfect nature,
    and an intensifying faith.

You took lemons
    and made the sweetest lemonade.
Thus,
    I do not thirst.

LONNETTA RAGLAND

I am full
    because you poured out and into me.
I am the result
    of your pleas with God.

Yes, you are indeed a mother
    in the truest sense of the word.
And I call you blessed
    and more than I could ever ask God for.
And if every woman loved their children the way you love yours,
    the world would be a different space.

The unforgettable flow of Pac tunes into my truth,
    "ain't a woman alive that can take my momma's place."

COALS FROM THE *Altar*

RESTING IN HIS ARMS

When the days' worry tries to steal my songs of praise,
    love draws me in Your direction.
Though this distress is a persistent devil,
    You pursue me with vigor.
Restlessness becomes the cradle that rocks me,
    until I find rest in You.
Your embrace assures me
    not one of my problems is bigger than You.
And when frustration tries to pick up where worry left off,
    You still me to your sovereign grace.
You remind me that you are God
    and I am not.
You remind me that you are on my side
    and while I don't have the answers, You do.
My Provision,
    if I have you, then I have everything I need.
And I journey off to retreat in You,
    the song in my heart and the reason why I sing.

III.

Revelation

Of everything I've accomplished, of everything I have gained, I count it as worthless, compared to the infinite valu, the priceless privilege of knowing Christ Jesus.

—Philippians 3:7–8, author's paraphrase

THE CHILDREN WITH BURNING HEARTS

(Inspired by A. W. Tozier)

Inception point
   but a flicker.
Others stand oblivious,
   living in permanent blink.
Nonetheless the combustible invisible
   shelters divine reaction between redemption and renovation.
New life ignites
   making the concealed manifest.
The flames range,
   lesser to engulfing.
Dimensions modulate,
   yet undeniably, equally real.

Sparks fly between crimson and golden,
   as they tango in the fullness of joy and pleasures forevermore.
Consecrated blazes generate heat
   the world can't afford to extinguish.
So with intensified mission,
   the children illume in adoration supreme.
They mount burning hearts
   on the altar.
Consumed by the Consuming Fire,
   the end to this seek gains no cognizance.
Absent the reek of smoke,
   yet radiating fragrance of eternity.
Sizzling pursuit to behold,
   the One for whom they live ignited.

COALS FROM THE *Altar*

YHWH

I AM WHO I AM,
 You are everything we need.
I AM WHO I AM,
 You are all-sufficiency.
There is none other,
 no one compares.
Created every created thing
 by declaring them into existence.
The only uncreated;
 deity exceeds human entreat for evidence.
Cares beyond our limits
 and abundant in mercy cloaked in patience.
Everywhere
 at once.
Incomparable
 and immutable.
Nothing more epic
 than the fact that God is.

While men mis-engineer the reality of You,
 proliferating rebellious heresy.
Man-made tools fail
 to disassemble the Spirit Divine.
Hateful hearts twist Your Word,
 maliciously employ to oppress.
Yet love
 is the mark of belonging to You.

LONNETTA RAGLAND

PARTOUT

Among the stars
 on a lucid midnight sky.
In the smell of fresh snow
 high on mountain tops.
In the golden cascades
 of balding trees.
Under the loose sands of the Sahara,
 in the infinite blanket that surrounds.
On scorching sun days
 and after a cool splash of ocean's blue.
In the depth of the Atlantic
 and its most celestial tide.
In the ripples of crowds,
 in the melodies of heartbeats.
In the stories that comprise life
 and the breeze of this moment.
You are everywhere,
 and yet we still miss you.

Coals from the Attar

HORIZON

Above the windowpane
   gazing through squinting grit.
Miles and miles of azure
   motion across the limitless vast.
Shuffling crowd of billions
   camouflage path potentials
Searching
   with a compromised compass.
Heart blue
   yet steadfast.
Rapidly standing still
   and knowing.
Running from exasperation's grasp,
   catapulted by a determination irreversible.
In the distance,
   I am now close enough to see.
You are immeasurable
   and beyond sight's capacity.

LONNETTA RAGLAND

RELENTLESS

Towers above paradise,
    the iridescent blue, its footstool.
Outruns the Nile,
    and reaches deeper than ocean's heels.
Boundless beyond seven galaxies,
    and wider than a proud mother's smile.
Shines brighter than the sun,
    able to carry through the darkest of days.
Doesn't need to clock out,
    because this love is evermore.

COALS FROM THE *Altar*

HARMONY IN A DRY PLACE

Oasis in the desert,
    thriving water that assuages beyond the paunch.
The exclusive heir of praise
    exceeding the sands of the earth.
The muse of worship
    that flourishes amidst aridity.
Hope that hovers the waves of epochs,
    and swathes during moonlit nightfall.
The One who holds the lyrics
    with a Mighty right hand.
Then like a rushing wind,
    blows on this orifice an exceptional melody.
As one, we orchestrate
    the kaleidoscope of holy devotion.
A ubiquitous harmony,
    even in this parched land.

LONNETTA RAGLAND

AT DAWN

In the stirring stillness of dawn
   my essence heeds Your unfailing affections.
Decluttering the shades of morning haze,
   searching for a place to visit with Your thoughts.
Debunking false evidence appearing real;
   vindicating horizon's tapestry making way for the Son's illumine.
Watching over me with a good father's heart,
   imparting wisdom to discern fox from sheep.
Cleansing windows clouded by the dew
   and unlocking seal to a common nightingale symphony.
Interceding in native tongue
   that I would make room for life abundant.

In the stirring stillness of dawn,
   curiosity moves me like a clock in reverse.
One set of footprints I meet in snow's deep;
   Yours.
Carrying me sound
   into the day's broken terrain.
And vociferously I profess
   forever to journey with You.

Coals from the Altar

GARDEN REGENERATION

Every weed deeply rooted in the feral garden of this soul
    excavated by the Master Gardener.
Clarified the design of my estate
    and planted seeds with veracity.
Dimensions conspicuous
    like stifling summer sun ray beams on a brow.
No more buying inputs
    based on someone else's blueprint.
Green thumb cultivated
    the soil of my heart.
Radiance exposed
    elderly wildflowers obscured from pruning.
Love nourished vital shoots
    to withstand undeniable pests and gales.
And commandment reversed
    the drought restricting growth.
Rained words
    that invigorated the inner most..

To behold,
    dead leaves trimmed away.
Once barren,
    now in full bloom.
In You, I abide
    and You, in me.
Together,
    we will bear much fruit.

LONNETTA RAGLAND

ABBA

Transcendent representation
    of the intended paternal design.
As the sea,
    arms wide.
Disciplines with affection,
    secures with principles.
Establishes your identity,
    erroneous decision never a possibility.
Rooted in trustworthiness,
    centered on you, His beloved.
Keeps close proximity,
    listening even when disregarded.
Serves as a place of rest,
    during sleepless epochs.
Protects,
    like any good father would.
Speaks purpose to the heart
    with loving affirmation.

COALS FROM THE *Attar*

EXTOL

Akin to a volcano
    seconds before it erupts.
Identical to a geyser
    primed to explode.
Too hard to contain,
    control is a distant companion.
Like the sand pebbles
    on Praia de Cassino.
Like the footsteps
    to journey from north to south.
So are the reasons
    to express what is due only to One.
Identical to the infinite rush of the Niagara,
    so is this praise.

LONNETTA RAGLAND

EXCLUSIVE

Exclusive covenant,
    no room for another.
Statues fail to compare,
    created by man's hands.
Lurking vessels frequent,
    tempting hasty hedonism of spiritual adultery.

But Your loyalty likens a magnet,
    and Your presence is heaven.
Covering me with an amazing love,
    an unconditional dynamic this world cannot replicate.
Eclipsing limitations;
    so grateful this type of love doesn't depend on me.
Leading me with resolve too divine to fathom,
    maturing in each minute we spend.
Counseling me through righteous wisdom,
    protecting from dangers this soul's window can't project.
Never operating in monotony,
    You make all things new.
Promises honored,
    grounded in redemptive intention.
You consistently love me,
    even beyond my inconsistency.

In an agitated ocean,
    Your gift of free will is anchored.
A glimpse beyond the horizon is unnecessary,
    You are the only choice.
None other before You,
    no one beside You.
My first love,
    to whom I vow faithfulness.
Because You have been that
    and exceedingly more to me.

COALS FROM THE *Altar*

INDIGO BRIDGES

Greeted by a mélange of sparkling retorts
   from their raised brows and side eyes
   to straight lips and private colloquies.

Can't omit the moment of silence
   and smooth genre transitions
   when I attempt to share how You transformed me.

When I try to express
   what You sounded like
   when You said my new name.

When I endeavor
   to convey how You led me
   to conviction and truth.

When I wear
   a smile with the joy
   that only comes from Your presence.

When I effort
   to tell them You love them
   more than they could ever grasp.

Maybe it's my choice of words,
   perhaps it is my delivery?
   Who am I that You would make me Your diplomat?

In trepidation
   I step out again on faith's indigo bridge
   and walk in love's obedience.

You give me courage
   not too soon
   and not too late.

LONNETTA RAGLAND

To open my mouth,
    speak what you inspire me to speak
    whether they choose to listen or not.

For eternal sunrises I will reverence You
    enough for them and me,
        until they want to do it on their own.

COALS FROM THE *Altar*

LOVE'S STAGE

Oh Immanuel,
    let our love be a stage for Your glory.
A constant advertisement of all that You are
    and all that You desire to be in the resolutions of Your people.
An inspiration for seeds to be planted in the depths of Your liberty
    growing the fruit of faithfulness.
Your love hung higher than the highest expectations,
    undeniably shining perfect light in the murk.
Evil will never undo
    the good You have done.
On this stage,
    I bask in Your brilliance.
On this stage,
    I pray for Your face to radiate upon ours.

LONNETTA RAGLAND

NO COMPARISON

If one is to boast,
    it could be me.
Several dozen semesters of academia,
    yielding six degrees.
I've got the house, family and career,
    some might say I'm living the American dream.

I've got plenty for me and mine,
    with enough to bless the next.
My reputation is solid;
    built on a foundation of mutual respect.

My executive suite flaunts scenic views from the 103rd floor,
    and is adorned with tokens of efforts recognized.
But of all the things I have accomplished or gained,
    nothing compares to the infinite value of knowing Christ.

Falling in love with Jesus
    is the best thing I've ever done.
Yet, I mustn't exaggerate
    the part I played in this divine occasion.

SUP WITH ME

Discombobulated what I saw when I looked in the mirror,
    stirred up questions I never thought to inquire.
The stride of my youth changed pace,
    and my speech carried a more spirited tone.
Favored past times of my mind's playground disappeared
    one by one.
The appeal of my eyes wasn't so any more
    and desires transformed with fresh attributes.
In response to all this movement,
    my arms raised towards the heavens.
My eyes closed in awe
    as the revelation of Abba picked me up.

You told me dining under the table was not my destiny
    and gifted me with new taste buds.
You invited me to sup with You
    and lovingly called me daughter.

LONNETTA RAGLAND

A PSALM FOR ONE

On this heart I build an altar
    for the God who saved my life.
He is due worship and reverence
    without apportioning.
The irrefutable Creator of Heaven and Earth,
    infinitely beyond our ability to understand.
Bigger than any problem,
    nothing is too hard for the Omnipotent.
Able to do anything,
    but fail.
Knew me before I knew myself,
    and formed me with intention.
Protected me while in my mother's womb
    and during the still of the night.
Even before I knew how to choose,
    the Adonai chose me.
Kept me,
    even when I didn't know I needed to be.
Hovered over,
    when I thought no one could see.
Heard my cries for help,
    though they couldn't break through hesitation.
While I spent years befriending idols,
    the God of forgiveness befriended me.
Didn't let me suffer
    the full consequences of the dark.
Walked me out of detrimental cycles
    before they amassed power to drown me.
Shined light on sinister places,
    then serenaded my soul's ear.
Schooled me about what love is
    and what it is not.

Jehovah Shalom comforted with peace and
    sustained me with His right hand.
In seeking more of Abba,
    I discovered myself.
Identity articulated
    only in connection to El-Shaddai.
My redeemer
    and provision.
In my heart,
    a void only the Trinity can fill.

Like David,
    such knowledge is too lofty to attain.
His loving correction
    shows that I can't follow Him and stay the same.

LONNETTA RAGLAND

IN THE EVENT OF...

Even if my name vanishes in obscurity
    and memories lose sight of my face;
Even supposing my faults outweigh the wins
    and mistakes birth irreconcilable damage;
Even now, if my words escape recall
    and my talents are perceived as naught;
Still, if my love wasn't enough
    and I could have done more, been more.

May they without delay,
    remember the Name of the One who I lived my life for.
The only Name
    the sun and stars obey.
The one Name
    that possesses the quench to every thirst.
The all-powerful Name
    that can regulate any storm.
Moves mountains
    and empowers quickening of feet.
Renews the mind
    and freely bestows new hearts.
Delivers the captives
    and can heal any disease.
Amazing affections beyond the constraints of humanity,
    and beyond description.

May they without delay
    remember the Name which is the sole constant
    in a world of perpetual shifts.
The Name of the One
    who consumed me with his fire.
The Name of the One
    who captured my heart until eternity's end.

EPILOGUE

I PRAY YOU ENJOYED *Coals from the Altar* and gleaned something that may deepen your personal relationship with God. I don't know how this book landed in your hands, but because it did, I know it's landing was purposeful!

I do not assume you have made the decision to invite Jesus into your heart and receive Him as Lord of your life. So, if you haven't, there is no better time than the present. It's easy to invite Him in. Just pray this simple prayer sincerely, and He will come in.

Dear God,

I admit I am a sinner. I have done many things that don't please You. I have lived my life for myself only. I am sorry, and I repent. I ask You to forgive me. I believe You died on the cross for me, to save me. You did what I could not do for myself.

I come to You now and I ask You to be Lord over my life. I surrender all to You. From this day forward, help me to live every day in a way that pleases You. Help me to walk in my true identity in You and the purposes You created me for.

I believe in You, Jesus, and I believe You want me to experience life and life more abundantly. I receive the brand-new life and fresh start that the

Bible promises that I can have. Lord, create in me a clean heart and renew a right spirit within me.

Thank You for forgiving me, redeeming me, and loving me. Thank You for new hope and love beyond anything I have ever known and the assurance of eternal life that is now mine.

In Your mighty name, amen.

If you just prayed for salvation for the first time, know that heaven is rejoicing over you! What to do now? Good next steps include:

- Find a Bible that is easy to read.

- Find a local church to connect with.

- Start talking with God in prayer regularly.

My child, pay attention to what I say. Listen carefully to my words. Don't lose sight of them. Let them penetrate deep into your heart, for they bring life to those who find them, and healing to their whole body. Guard your heart above all else, for it determines the course of your life.

—Proverbs 4:20–23

ABOUT THE AUTHOR

Lonnetta Ragland is communications and public relations strategist and freelance writer. She started composing poetry as a hobby and form of self-expression during her childhood.

She gave her life to Jesus in 2002. In subsequent years, God revealed Himself to her and allowed her to experience the supernatural weight of His presence. He awakened within her a desire to write not just professionally for corporate clients but also about journeying with Him over the years. These defining moments changed her life forever and led to her first book, *Coals from the Altar*.

She is passionate about using creative expression for God's glory. Active in church, community, and mentoring initiatives, she also loves quality time with friends and family, the arts, travel, and music. Lonnetta is also an avid student of health, fitness, and nutrition.

She holds degrees in mass communications and international development and health.

www.ingramcontent.com/pod-product-compliance
Lightning Source LLC
Chambersburg PA
CBHW012207090526
44583CB00022BA/2941